THE
Archive Photographs
SERIES

REIGATE
AND REDHILL

THE
Archive Photographs
SERIES

REIGATE
AND REDHILL

Compiled by
Mary G. Goss

*With thanks and
good wishes,
Mary G. Goss*

CHALFORD

The Chalford Publishing Company
St Mary's Mill, Chalford,
Stroud, Gloucestershire, GL6 8NX

ISBN 0 7524 0179 3

Typesetting and origination by
The Chalford Publishing Company
Printed in Great Britain by
Redwood Books, Trowbridge

One event which still goes on is the Old Crocks Rally from London to Brighton passing through Redhill. It is held to commemorate the ending of a rule which said that a motor car should be preceded by a man with a warning red flag. Here several cars are coming up the steep part of Brighton Road.

Contents

Acknowledgements

Surrey Local Studies Library, Redhill Library, Reigate Priory Museum, Holmesdale Natural History Club, Reigate, Bert Latham, Ernest Freeman, Eunice and Edward Hatt for allowing access to their post-card collections. Angela Alabaster, Nellie Basting, Ethel Bristow, Paul Buckland, Joy Caplin, Heloise Collier, D. Church, Peter Finch (Nutfield History Group), Jean Francis, Joyce Hooper, Giles Graham-Brown (Redland), Lens of Sutton, Maureen Pendered, Roland Rose, Jack Sale, Jennifer Smalley, David Thomas (Redhill Football Club), Leslie Wearn. Qualitext Business Services for processing the manuscript.

Bibliography

Dunne, Nigel   *The Redhill Story* (1994)
Hooper, Wilfred   *Reigate: Its Story through the Ages* (1945)

'The old order changes yielding place to new'. The old Yew Tree inn on Reigate Hill built of Reigate stone is yielding place to the new half-tiled building behind. The date on the new building is 1938.

Introduction

In 1863 when Reigate Parish became a Municipal Borough, there were two centres. Reigate, the old market town, grew up in the shadow of the Norman Castle while Redhill, two miles to the east, was a creation of the railway which came in 1841. Very different in character, they developed together throughout the nineteenth century not without rivalries which persist even today. In 1933 the Borough boundaries were extended to include Merstham and Gatton. The Monson family and later the Colmans of Gatton Hall had long been closely associated with the Borough. The population was then over 30,000. In 1974 the much larger Borough of Reigate and Banstead was created with a population of over 115,000.

The Borough is noted for its varied and attractive scenery which is closely related to geology. To the north are the North Downs made of chalk with a conspicuous south facing scarp slope. Immediately to the south of this is a narrow outcrop of Upper Greensand, a buff coloured sandy limestone which was extensively quarried in the past. There follows a vale of Gault clay about half a mile wide and beyond it a three mile wide ridge of Lower Greensand on which most of Redhill and Reigate are built. Redhill derives its name from the sands of Redhill Common which have a red tinge. The steep southern slopes of Redhill Common and Reigate Park drop down to the vale of Weald Clay below. The whole area is drained by tributaries of the River Mole which forms the Borough boundary on the south west.

Chapter 4 deals with the wide variety of open spaces enjoyed by the citizens of the Borough. Reigate Heath, Wray Common, Redhill and Earlswood Commons are all Common lands of the Manor. Traditionally, citizens had rights of grazing animals, gathering wood for fuel, and bracken for bedding their animals. None of these rights is exercised today and the Commons are used for formal and informal recreation. Other open spaces have been donated or purchased. The ending of grazing by farm stock and rabbits has led to encroachment of scrub and trees. The myxamatosis epidemic of the 1950s wiped out most of the rabbit population. Efforts are now being made to restore chalk grassland and lowland heath as important habitats for wild life.

Most of the old industries featured in Chapter 6 no longer exist. Service occupations now predominate. In the retail trade there are still a few family firms who resist the growth of multiple stores and supermarkets. Chapter 7 is a collection of pictures of people and events. The processions which were such a feature of life in the nineteenth and early twentieth centuries are no longer possible under modern traffic conditions.

Many of the pictures in this collection are the work of Francis Frith, the first man to exploit the commercial possibilities of photography. An Act of Parliament in 1897 removed restrictions on postage for picture postcards. Frith lived in Reigate and produced several hundred such cards. He tried to add human interest to scenes by featuring vehicles and people. Some of his nine children appeared frequently. Most of the pictures were taken between 1900 and 1914.

Before the days of photography, drawings, paintings and engravings were used to illustrate books. Many of these appeared later as picture postcards.

The Castle Steps link the Market Place with the Castle grounds and London Road beyond. This route was the main way to the north before the Tunnel Road was constructed.

One

Historic Reigate

Reigate Parish Church first mentioned in the twelfth century was built to serve the lost village of Cherchefelle. The nave and the south aisle are conspicuous in the foreground and a fourteenth century tower crowns the building. There was much restoration in the nineteenth century, the local stone being refaced by a more durable Bath Stone.

Reigate town grew up not round the Church but round the Castle built in 1088 soon after the Norman Conquest. It was formed by cutting a deep ditch round a hill and throwing the excavated soil onto a mound or motte. The original buildings were of timber but a curtain wall with fortifications was built in 1300.

In 1873 the Castle grounds were laid out as gardens. In the top centre of the picture is the entrance to a network of caves, probably used for storage.

Nothing of the old Castle survives but this gateway was erected in 1770 from stones gathered in the ruins.

A lofty cave called the Baron's Hall because it was erroneously believed to be where the Barons met before going to Runnymede for the signing of Magna Carta with King John.

An engraving of Reigate Priory as it was in 1577. It was founded in the thirteenth century for a small community of Augustinian or Black Canons Regular. At the Dissolution of the Monasteries in 1541, when only 4 canons remained, it was granted by the King to Lord William Howard who converted the buildings into a Tudor mansion.

Known now as the Old Town Hall, this building erected in 1729 was known as the New Market House as it replaced the old one at the west end of the town. Brick built on ten arches, it is surmounted by a cupola and clock tower. The four chimneys were added in 1853.

In 1766 much of the old structure was pulled down and the wings were reduced to shallow projections. A fine Georgian house resulted. In 1808 it was bought by Lord Somers whose family held it until 1921 as Lords of the Manor of Reigate.

The cage for prisoners used to stand near the Market Place but was moved in 1811 to a site south of the High Street and used as a workshop. It has been recently restored as part of the Safeway Store complex in Cage Yard.

At the west end of the High Street stands the Red Cross Hotel. There has been an Inn on this site since the Middle Ages. To its left is Slipshoe Street and between the two tile-hung buildings is West Street. Most of this has disappeared under road widening schemes.

The sole survivor of the old cottages shows the over-hang of the upper storey. The Red Cross can be seen at the end of the street.

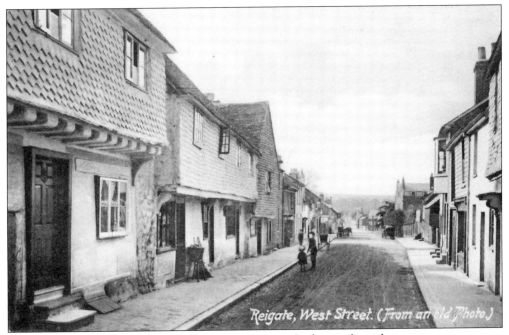

West Street as it was in 1910 looking west to Brownes Lodge on the right.

This modern picture is of Browne's Lodge which has shown little change since it was built in 1786 on a wedge-shaped site with a fine Cedar tree.

Further west is Old West Street House (1720) which once housed the National School. Next to it is the Old Forge which functioned until 1970.

Opposite the Red Cross, Park Lane leads to the west side of Priory Park. The house facing the camera was once the Workhouse. The children show the dress of 1900.

Facing the Market Square is the White Hart Hotel in Bell Street. This 1894 picture shows a coach en route from Brighton to London. Horses were changed here. It was demolished in 1935.

Queen Victoria passed this way soon after her accession in 1837. This triumphal arch was erected outside the White Hart.

This ancient building next to the White Hart is the site of St Lawrence's Chapel dating from the fourteenth century.

Old buildings on the west side of Bell Street include Chandler's butcher shop and the Grapes Hotel.

Next door to Knights is the Old Post Office with its pillar box.

A closer view of the Grapes Hotel and Knight's store which took it over in 1911.

Bell Street looking north to the Market Square in 1900. The new Post Office on the left was demolished in 1992 to make way for the Safeway development. Outside is the horse-drawn van of Keasleys, the bakers, who had many branches in the district.

Church Street looking west to the Old Town Hall. None of these buildings remain. Over the wall on the left are the grounds of The Barons.

A striking feature of the town is the Tunnel Road which was cut through the Castle grounds in 1843 to avoid a detour round the Castle. Adams stores in the corner of Church Street can be seen on the right and the Market Hotel on the left.

A modern picture of The Barons recently restored by Redlands. A Queen Anne house of 1710 it was the home of Baron Maseres, a wealthy man of Huguenot origin.

The other side of the Tunnel shows the steep wooded slopes. Here the many coloured sands of the Lower Greensand can be clearly seen.

In 1824 a cutting was made in the chalk at the top of Reigate Hill to improve the gradient of the road from London. A suspension foot-bridge was constructed above it. This was replaced in 1910 by a stronger bridge.

The Toll-gate, Reigate Hill.

At the foot of Reigate Hill, a Toll-gate was built. On the left is the toll house where money was collected for the upkeep of the road. Next to it is the Yew Tree Inn built in 1841. Behind is the chalk quarry and a stretch of open downland now much overgrown by scrub.

South of Reigate at Woodhatch there was another Toll-gate near the Angel Hotel (1650). The hotel was supplied by the local Brewery, Mellersh & Neal.

Two
Early Redhill and the Coming of the Railway

What is now Redhill was a rural area with scattered farms and hamlets. Much of the site was low lying and marshy, drained by the Brook and its tributaries. In this picture the Brook is crossed by a foot-bridge close to Copyhold Cottage.

The Brook was subject to flooding as seen in this 1969 picture. It is now culverted for most of its length.

Redhill, Cottages at foot of Batt's Hill.

Another group of cottages in Linkfield Lane has been much photographed. This picture taken in 1900 shows them covered in creeper which has been removed to reveal the half-timbered construction beneath.

One of the hamlets was Linkfield Street. This eighteenth century tile-hung cottage looks derelict but has now been restored.

The old road from Reigate to Nutfield and beyond ran along the edge of Redhill Common and down Mill Street - shown in this 1907 picture.

A modern picture of a restored timber framed cottage in Mill Street.

The road in this picture is Brighton Road opened in 1816 from Gatton Point as an alternative route to that through Reigate. The building on the left at the junction of Mill Street is an attractive Regency House which was an Inn called the Somers Arms. It is now a residence called The Firs.

This rural scene shows the Marquis of Granby in Mill Street with the slopes of Redstone Hill behind. Just beyond the Inn, the road crossed the Brook where is was thought a Mill was situated.

Another hamlet was known as Little London consisting largely of the cottages of squatters on the lower slopes of Redhill Common. In 1843 St John's Church was built to serve the needs of the people of the eastern districts of Reigate Parish.

Beyond St John's is Earlswood Common where Lord Somers granted land for the building of a Workhouse shown in this 1821 picture. It later became Redhill General Hospital - closed in 1987. A new housing estate is being built on the site.

In 1841 the London, Brighton and South Coast Railway Company opened a line from London Bridge to Brighton and a year later, the South East Railway Company constructed a line from Redhill to Tonbridge and Dover. In 1849 the line to Reigate, Guildford and Reading was opened, thus creating a large station known as Reigate Junction - shown in the picture. The steam train is leaving on the Tonbridge line while the Brighton line is in the centre. The line to Reigate leaves on the left. This artist's impression shows a growing settlement.

The North Downs were breached by a tunnel at Merstham, over a mile long. Air shafts can be seen on the top of the tunnel which is approached by a deep cutting.

Redhill Junction's complex lines seen from the south. Beyond the platform on the right is the Post Office Sorting Office, established in 1884 as a Forwarding Centre for an area bounded by London, Brighton and Dover, Reading.

Re-named Redhill Junction, the station is seen from the foot-bridge on the north side. Railway workers cottages can be seen on the right.

Disputes between the two Railway Companies led the London, Brighton & South Coast Company to construct another line from Coulsdon North to Earlswood. A second Merstham tunnel was needed and a tunnel through the Lower Greensand made it possible to by-pass Redhill. Six miles long without any stations, it is known as the Quarry Line. Shown in the picture is the Brighton Belle, consisting of Pullman coaches.

Reigate had its station on the Reading line, less convenient for travellers to London who often had to change at Redhill. This picture shows the level crossing with the gates closed to allow the train to pass. Always an obstacle, it creates serious congestion under modern traffic conditions.

The gardens at Reigate Station were always well kept in contrast to the neglect of today. The dog called Jack had a box on his back to collect for the Railwayman's Convalescent Homes.

London Road, Reigate, in 1900, with a view across the level crossing to the chalk pits on Reigate Hill. The buildings on the left were mainly shops but were replaced by offices, now housing the Surrey Mirror.

NED JULY 21, 1858.

BAPTIST CHAPEL, STATION ROAD RED HILL, SURREY.

FROM A SKETCH BY T. R. }

This sketch by T. R. Hooper shows the Baptist Chapel in Station Road built in 1858 on land leased from the S.E. Railway Company. It still stands surrounded by shops. The beginnings of a settlement called Warwick Town can be seen.

Further up the road was the Warwick Hotel at the corner of Warwick Road. The land was leased from the Countess of Warwick, widow of the fourth Lord Monson, who lived at Gatton Park. St Matthew's Church, built in 1866, can be seen in the distance.

The centre of Redhill was this cross-roads with the High Street on the left and London Road on the right. Station Road runs through the middle of the picture which dates from 1900.

On the west side of the High Street are some well-known shops - Jones and Berrett were drapers and outfitters, while in between was S. C. Jennings, Stationers & Printers. On the east side was Gatlands Clothing stores and the entrance to the Market.

At the corner of Station Road East and London Road, the Redhill Market House Company erected a Corn Exchange in 1857. A west wing was added in 1891 to house the Post Office until 1932. The east wing was added in 1903. The Assembly Rooms in the main building were used for functions of all kinds, including dramas. The building was demolished in 1982 to make way for the new Warwick Quadrant. Note the continuation of the name Warwick.

In 1887, land was bought by the Borough Council from the S.E. Railway Company for a Stock Market. A more general market with amusements was held on Saturdays. In 1895, Reigate Market was closed; the function of market town having passed to Redhill. This market has been long closed and is now a car park. The retail market was revived recently in a pedestrianised High Street.

Looking down Station Road East to the railway bridge. On the corner with the High Street is Nichols, another drapers and outfitters which was destroyed in a disastrous fire in 1901 but rebuilt in the same style soon after. A small Sainsbury's is next door.

London Road looking towards the High Street. None of this remains having given way to the Warwick Quadrant development. On the right is the Queen's Arms and next to it, H&A Trowers, Corn & Seed merchants. On the left a cab is outside Rose's fruit shop and the awning further on denotes the position of Smith's China shop with the Market Hall beyond.

A tree-lined London Road continues northwards past the Colman Institute given to the town by Sir Jeremiah Colman of Gatton. It offered educational and recreational facilities. Beyond on the right is the Sports Ground.

A game of Cricket is in progress and a young mother relaxes with her family. Redhill Football Club used the ground for most of its history. It is now a public park. St Anne's School is conspicuous in the background.

There was little development east of Redhill Station in the nineteenth century. The Reigate Junction Hotel was built soon after the railway came and re-named Lakers Hotel in 1904 after the family who owned it. Cottages for railway workers are seen on the left. Redstone Hill was built to join the station to the old road to Nutfield and has since become the main road (A25).

Redhill extended southwards along the Brighton Road. In the background can be seen the spire of the Roman Catholic Church and the Reading Arch which carries the railway across the road. The gas works were later re-located in Hooley Lane, part of the old road. The steepness of the gradient is because Lord Somers would not allow the road to follow the easier route along the Brook Valley later taken by the railway.

Three

The Borough Grows

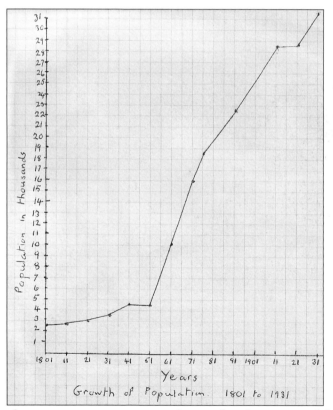

Growth of Population. 1801 to 1931

The graph shows the enormous increase in population after the coming of the railway, the greatest growth being between 1851 and 1871. This led Reigate Parish to seek borough status in 1864 to organise the provision of services.

A view from the tower of Reigate Parish Church in 1910 shows the scarp of the North Downs with the Pilgrims' Way and the beech woods as a back-drop to the growing town. The railway crosses the middle of the picture. Conspicuous in the middle is Reigate Lodge set in extensive grounds. It was demolished in 1920 to make way for housing development and the County School for Girls. New housing in the bottom right hand corner is on the site of another great house, Great Doods.

Great Doods. A Victorian Mansion in extensive grounds was sold for re-development in 1906.

A view of Redhill from the slopes of the Common in 1895. The North Downs are in the background and St. Anne's School can be seen beyond the railway. Mill Street is in the foreground.

The road which linked Reigate to Redhill rises to the left of the early nineteenth century house called Delville, now the home of the headmaster of the Grammar School further up the hill.

Shaw's Corner where Redhill and Reigate meet. The Presbyterian Church was built in 1904. The chestnut tree was cut down to make way for the War Memorial. (see Chapter 7)

At the top of the hill, this 1857 Friends Meeting House was built on the site of an older building (1688). The Friends were the first non-conformist sect in the Borough. This building has now been replaced by a smaller modern meeting house and retirement flats.

Between Shaw's Corner and Redhill is Linkfield Corner. There is a variety of shops run by families who lived over them. The buildings on either side of the road in this 1915 picture still remain but the group in the middle has given way to a large traffic roundabout.

To the south of Redhill, Earlswood grew up round another station on the Brighton line. The Station Hotel can be seen on the right. The Methodist Chapel is now a mosque catering for the growing Asian community.

In St. John's parish is Meadvale, once a hamlet called Mead Hole. It developed in the nineteenth century when people were employed in a tannery and brick works. Its main street, called Somerset Road, is seen in this picture. Keaseley's van is delivering bread.

St. John's Church was rebuilt in 1889. Its tall spire is a striking local landmark. The area round the church has many old stone cottages and is now a Conservation Area.

Further up the road is the Post Office at the corner of Copse Road. There were many more shops in 1905 than there are today.

Reigate was also growing. Holmesdale Road grew up outside the Station. The Railway Hotel has now been replaced by an office block. The 'Prince of Wales' seen in the distance still stands.

Nutley Lane is an old road which led from the old Market Place to the hill. St. Philip's Church seen in the centre was built in 1863 to cater for working class people who were mainly employed in the large houses. This scene shows little change today.

St. Mark's Church was built in 1860 to meet the needs of the growing population, north of the railway. The spire was removed in 1900 as it was unsafe. The adjacent Vicarage has been replaced by a modern house.

A closer view of Beehive Stores, a typical corner shop, still serving the needs of the community.

This familiar scene taken about 1930 shows that horse-drawn traffic has given way to bicycles, motorcars and buses. The signposts are at the junction of the east-west A25 and the north-south A217. The Tunnel road, now pedestrianised, carried traffic both ways.

An open-topped bus of the East Surrey Traction Company ran between Reigate and Redhill.

This bus in Church Street is outside the gates of Reigate Lodge. The cottages on the right were replaced by a garage which later made way for offices. The road on the left is Castlefield Road, constructed in 1900 to serve the new Municipal Buildings built on the Castle fields.

Municipal Buildings, Reigate.

Municipal Buildings. On the left is the new Fire Station and on the far right the Law Courts. The central part housed the Council Chamber and local government offices. Now called the Town Hall, many more buildings have been erected on the site. The field on the right was used for housing.

Burtenshaw's Garage in West Street, established in the reign of George III, made carriages, traps and shooting brakes drawn by horses. With the coming of motor cars, they made car bodies for Daimlers. They became engineers and car agents. Two petrol pumps can be seen in the picture.

An early taxi outside Redhill Station. Pattersons had virtual monopoly of the taxi trade between the Wars.

Merstham Pond and Church.

In 1934, the Borough boundaries were extended to include Merstham and Gatton. Merstham Church is seen in the trees beyond the pond which is one of the sources of the Redhill Brook. It is fed by springs which emerge at the foot of the chalk hills.

A closer view of the thirteenth century Church which is built of flint found in the chalk. The Church is now cut off from the village by the M25.

The centre of the village in 1900. The Post Office and Chapel stand side by side.

Quality Street flanked by picturesque cottages of various dates. It is called after a play by J. M. Barrie in which Seymour Hicks and his wife, Ellaline Terris, appeared.

The Hicks lived at the Old Forge. The half timbered gable on the left dates from the fifteenth century but the half-tiled house is mainly eighteenth century.

Gatton Hall, the home of the Monson family, has a conspicuous site on the upper greensand ridge. An early nineteenth century classical style house, it lies in spacious landscaped grounds with many lakes.

A closer view of the north side of the Hall. The ten marble Corinthian columns with a limestone pediment date from 1891.

St. Andrew's Church, Gatton. This thirteenth century Church was re-modelled by Lord Monson on his return from the Grand Tour. Like a museum, it housed his collections.

The fifth Baron Monson (son of the Countess of Warwick) who had done the Grand Tour was responsible for the creation of the Marble Hall with materials sent from Italy. In 1888, the Estate was sold to the Colman family, makers of mustard in Norwich. In February 1923, a disastrous fire gutted the Hall which was rebuilt without the Marble Hall. No longer a residence, Gatton Hall is the main building of the Royal Alexander & Albert School.

The interior of Gatton Church showing the elaborate wood carvings.

This open Doric Temple with six iron columns called Gatton Town Hall was built in 1765 for the holding of "elections". Gatton was a Rotten Borough which sent two members to Parliament. As none of the 28 people on the Estate had a vote, the elections were nominations. This undemocratic procedure ended with the 1832 Reform Act.

Four
Open Spaces

Reigate Heath, Golf Club House.

Reigate Heath in the far west of the Borough has pale sandy soil which gives rise to lowland heath with heather, bracken and gorse predominating. However, encroachment by Birch is a serious problem. On the highest point is an eighteenth century Post Mill, several cottages and a Golf Club house, the balcony of which has since been removed.

The Mill ceased grinding in 1880 and the brick round-house was converted into a Chapel of ease for Reigate Parish Church. In 1962, the Mill was restored and new sails added to enhance its appearance.

Lady Henry Somerset, then Lord of the Manor, allowed the use of the heath for a golf course and she financed the Club House. A group of ladies is seen at the "pond hole" in 1919. The pond is no longer a permanent feature as the water table has fallen. In very wet years, such as 1997, it re-appears. Reigate Park and Bonny's mineral water works can be seen in the background.

Inside the Chapel. The central post has been cut away but the massive side beams remain.

Cottages along Flanchford Road. Most of these have been improved or rebuilt in an attractive setting facing the Heath.

A Tower Mill on Wray Common which worked from 1824 to 1895. Its sails have gone and it is now a residence. This Common is on clay and was used for cattle pasture in this 1900 picture.

The road from Reigate to east Surrey ran from Shaw's Corner along the edge of Redhill Common and down Mill Street. White Post House seen on the left, housed Redhill's first Post Office.

This is a modern picture of Wray Farm House from which the area now known as Wray Park was farmed. It has been restored to make an attractive residence, mainly of brick and tiles, but some Reigate stone has been used.

Redhill Common rises up to the crest of the lower greensand ridge. The pillar on the top was used for sighting by the railway engineers. It was replaced by a direction indicator in 1935, in memory of a former Mayor. The Common was more open early in the century than it is today.

Redhill Common

This round pond was constructed to water the cattle from the nearby farm. Children later enjoyed sailing their boats and catching tadpoles. In the 1930s it was concreted, thus destroying some of its natural attraction. A modern restoration project is being carried out by volunteers.

The Pond, Earlswood Redhill   E.Frank Millen

Earlswood Common to the south is low lying land on Weald Clay. Trees and grass prevail. There are two ponds separated by a wooden footbridge. On the right is New Pond or Lower Lake which dates from the fourteenth century. On the left is the Upper Lake created from clay excavations for a nearby brick works.

On the side of the Common above Mill Street there had been extensive quarrying for building stone. This ceased when a local citizen challenged the right to do this on Common land. What was called "Pleasure Gardens" were laid out to provide recreational facilities for the growing local population. Here a game of tennis is in progress on the level floor of a quarry. Today, there is no sign of formal pleasure gardens, the land having reverted to the Common.

BATHING POOL, EARLSWOOD LAKE, REDHILL.   H.8870.

New Pond was once a popular bathing place but it is now stocked with fish and bathing is no longer allowed.

Earlswood Lake, The Island

After the first World War, the upper lake was further excavated to create a boating lake. An island was created in the centre. The canoes and rowing boats seen in the picture were available for hire.

The steep paths up the chalk scarp and the road leading to them are called "The Pilgrims' Way" once believed to be part of the route taken by pilgrims going to the shrine of Thomas à Becket at Canterbury. Houses can be seen in the picture and there was fear that more housing would encroach on the hill. There were many fund-raising efforts to save the hill. To this end, in 1913 the Pilgrims Pageant was held (see Chapter 7). As a result of this and other efforts, the National Trust was able to buy Colley Hill.

The granite pillar, unveiled in 1910, commemorates the donation of nearly three acres of land by a benefactor in memory of her son.

This Drinking Fountain surrounded by 12 pillars was also given to the Borough by a benefactor. Inside the roof is a colourful mosaic of the firmament. Sadly, it has often been vandalised. A direction indicator has replaced the fountain.

A magnificent stand of Beech trees linked Colley Hill to Reigate Hill. Planted in the eighteenth century, they were severely damaged in the great gale of 1987. Replanting is proceeding but it will be many years before its former glory will be restored.

This is a view over Reigate to the lower greensand ridge in the distance. It must have been taken before 1900 as St. Mark's Church still has its spire. The fields below have been built over.

This view was taken near to where the main road crosses Reigate Hill. It had become obscured by tree growth but the great gale opened it up again.

Yet another public open space is Reigate Park on the lower greensand ridge, south of the Priory. It had wonderful views north, over Reigate town, and south over the Weald but growth of trees has largely obscured them.

The memorial to Mr Randall Vogan who gave Reigate Park to the Borough. In 1921 he also bought the Old Town Hall and presented it to the Borough Council.

Five

Schools and
Institutions

A "dame school" on Reigate Heath. Miss Weekly and her 20 pupils photographed outside the school in 1905. The boy in a sailor suit in the centre of the front row is five year old Henry Francis whose daughter, a retired headmistress, still lives on the Heath.

Reigate Grammar School. The original school house opened near the parish Church in 1664 with the Vicar as master. Its aim was to educate poor children in the principles of the Church of England. There were ten free places supported by endowments. The master was free to take in further pupils on his own terms. Growth was slow, numbers reaching 36 by 1870.

A football eleven posing outside the main entrance in 1922. Originally a boy's school, it now takes in girls.

In 1871, the headmaster's house and a new school room, built of Reigate stone, can be seen on the left. A few years later, a Board of Governors took over the school, ten of the fourteen members being elected by the Borough Council. The main building to the right of the picture was erected in 1907. Subsequent extensions have created a school for 800 pupils. It is now an independent fee-paying school, a far cry from the original intentions of the founders.

There were no comparable facilities for girls who were educated in the elementary schools, private schools, or at home. In 1899, the Church Schools Company opened Reigate High School in Somers Road, near the Station. Twenty years later it closed and the buildings were taken over by Micklefield School.

Redhill, Technical Institute &c.

Redhill Technical Institute was built at the foot of Redstone Hill, near the Station in 1895 for the study of Arts and Sciences. Classes were mainly in the evenings, until 1926, when a junior department was opened. One of the classes was for pupils in the elementary schools who wished to become teachers. Many of those went on to Teacher Training Colleges.

In 1908, the girls moved to Gore House in Cavendish Road, the boys having transfered to the Grammar School. Gore House is seen on the left of the picture. Clyde House next door was acquired in 1919. Scholarships were available for children from the elementary schools and fee-paying pupils were admitted.

Miss Anderton, the first headmistress, and the staff of Reigate County School for Girls in 1921.

Miss Anderton, Miss McAllister and the girls of the Upper Vth in 1921. Most of these girls became teachers.

In 1927, the school moved to a brand new building in the grounds of Reigate Lodge (see Chapter 3). Now Reigate College, the site contains many more buildings. Rushworth Road is at the top of the picture and at the bottom are new houses in South Walk.

The staff of Reigate County School in 1932. Miss Aitken, the headmistress is in the centre with her deputy, Miss Burchell, on her right and Miss Crook, an old girl of the school on her left. Miss Lewis (third from left on back row) is the only member of staff who appears in the 1921 photograph.

The British School moved from a site in Reigate High Street to this site in Holmesdale Road. It, too, is due to move to a new building, in Alma Road.

Elementary education in the early nineteenth century was provided by the National Society, a Church of England organisation and the British and Foreign School Society which was mainly non-conformist. This modern picture shows Reigate Parish School which moved from West Street to this site in London Road in 1854. In 1995, it moved to a new site in Blackborough Road and housing will take its place.

A group of girls from Holmesdale School after a Netball match about 1900. The school catered for boys and girls up to the age of 14.

A class at Frenches Road School, Redhill, in 1925. One of the schools established as a result of the Education Act of 1870 when School Boards were set up to increase the number of places which the voluntary societies were unable to provide.

A nursery class for children from 3 to 5 at Cromwell Road School, Redhill, in 1962. Established between the Wars, nursery schools and classes were not a compulsory part of the education system. The children learned through play.

The coming of the Railway made it possible for institutions to move out from London to more spacious surroundings. The first to come was the Philanthropic Society which ran a home in London for destitute children to train them for a trade. Land was bought from the S.E. Railway Company in 1849. This artist's impression shows the Warden's house on the left which still stands and the Chapel and two residences on the right which have been replaced by modern buildings. In 1854, the aim of the school was to cure boys who were committed to a criminal life. To training in workshops was added training in farming. Of the five houses with 50 boys in each, some were set amongst fields. Known as the Philanthropic Farm School, it was first supported by voluntary subscriptions but later received government grants. In the twentieth century, it was gradually run down and closed in 1988. It is now a training school run by the National Institute for the Blind.

In 1856, the Earlswood Asylum for Idiots was built on land, east of the Brighton line near Earlswood Station. Greatly enlarged after 1870, by 1900 it had 600 residents and 150 attendants. Under the present policy of "Care in the Community" it is about to close. The grounds were so extensive that it was possible to build the new East Surrey Hospital on part of them.

St. Anne's School, Redhill.

A conspicuous feature of the Redhill sky-line was St. Anne's School which moved from London to land east of Redhill Station in 1884. Its aim was to feed, clothe and educate children from families in reduced circumstances. The headmaster and his deputy were both Church of England clergymen. The girls were educated separately. Constant fund-raising was necessary to keep the school going but it was forced to close in 1919. The building on the right is the Chapel, while the main building is crowned by a Clock Tower which could be seen and heard for miles around.

From 1926 to 1937, St Anne's was taken over by the Foundling Society who catered for abandoned children. The children wore distinctive brown uniform. The boys' waistcoats were red which earned them the name "robin redbreasts". The boy is carrying a bugle so perhaps he was a member of the band.

Facing Redhill Common, the Reigate & Redhill Hospital was built in 1910. Local doctors treated their own patients here in co-operation with appointed staff. In 1923, it was re-named East Surrey Hospital. After the retirement of the last G.P. surgeon, work gradually passed to the Redhill General Hospital on the old workhouse site. In 1984, the New East Surrey Hospital was opened. The site of Redhill General Hospital is being developed for housing.

Six

Occupations

There are still farms in and around the Borough but they are highly mechanised and give work to few people today. Here a man is seen guiding the horse-drawn plough which turns the soil over ready for planting the seed.

A mechanised reaper binder cutting the Corn below Colley Hill. It cut the Corn and bound it into stooks.

Hay-making. This machine tosses the cut grass to help to dry it.

A steam-driven threshing machine separates the grain from the ear. Today the work of both machines is done by a combine harvester.

Horse-drawn carts have brought the hay to the stack. The hay was used to feed the animals throughout the Winter.

Old maps show a farm called Wiggie to the north of what is now Redhill. Fifty acres in extent, it had arable land, meadows, orchards and vegetable gardens, as well as stock. The farm was cut up by the railway lines, so A&H Trower went into business as millers, corn & seed merchants. What was left of the land became a famous garden opened to the public in the Spring to see a magnificent display of daffodils. The Victorian house is seen in the background.

A feature of the area is the number of nursery gardens, such as Well's Nursery between Redhill and Merstham. Here, Chrysanthemum cuttings are being planted out in a large greenhouse.

In this picture, Jennifer is arranging a group of prize Chrysanthemums for exhibition. The Nursery closed in 1962 and the site is used for warehousing.

Wonham Mill, a water mill on a tributary of the River Mole, owned by A&H Trower. Sacks of wheat are brought by large horse-drawn carts. The buildings are still there but milling ceased long ago.

Local Public Houses also served Bonny's mineral waters produced at this works on Reigate Heath. From 1887 to 1957 abundant pure water was available from a deep well sunk into the lower greensand. Bonny's cottage, the home of the Proprietor is seen on the left, while to the right off the picture are ten cottages built for the workers. Modern houses now occupy the factory site.

Local Barley was used for brewing Ale. A fleet of delivery vans is seen in the yard of Mellersh and Neale's brewery, about 1920. The brewery tower was demolished recently to make way for the Safeway Supermarket.

Also on the Heath was a stonemason's business founded in 1860 by Mr Henry Francis who made monuments for graveyards. A horse-drawn cart brought the stone from Reigate Station. Granite from Scotland and Cornwall, and marble from Italy were used.

The varied geology of the Borough gave rise to many extractive industries, none of which is active today. Chalk was used to produce lime for fertiliser and cement. Below the chalk, the upper greensand yielded a stone used for building since the Middle Ages. Often called Reigate stone, it was obtained by tunnelling. A network of caves like this extends from Dorking to the Kent border.

The stone which can be seen in the walls of Churches and other buildings weathers easily and is no longer used for building. However, mining went on until 1961 producing Hearthstone from a softer band. It was used all over the country as a scouring stone. On the left of the picture are the rough stones brought out of the tunnel while the trimmed blocks are seen on the cart. Behind are wooden pit props which supported the roof. The rail track took the stone to a siding on the railway for distribution.

This picture is of great significance, for the Redland Company which now has operations in over 30 countries, began its life here. The Redhill Tile Company started making concrete tiles in this old quarry at the foot of Redstone Hollow in 1921. The Company's head office is still in Reigate at the corner of Castlefield Road.

In the lower greensand, east of Redhill occur seams of Fuller's Earth, a clay of soapy consistency which was first used in the woollen industry for cleaning the wool and finishing the cloth. In the twentieth century, new uses were found particularly in the refining of oils, both vegetable and mineral. This picture taken in 1900, shows the workers with picks, shovels, and wheelbarrows, working on flexible planks. Later, the extraction was done by machines and fewer men were employed. The deposits are now worked out.

An important industry in Redhill was the Tannery in Linkfield Street founded in the eighteenth century and closed in 1961. This picture shows the sheds just before they were demolished for the building of a housing estate.

An industry which once employed 2000 people in Redhill was the Monotype Corporation which came in 1901. They made all kinds of type from hot metal castings used for printing books and newspapers all over the world. The picture shows the original building.

The extensive Monotype works in 1970. By 1950, printing by the offset lithographic process had reduced the demand for Monotype casting machines, though export to Third World countries continues. The work force is now reduced to 200. Several printing works such as the Athenaeum, Surrey Fine Arts and Jennings used Monotype machines.

Many people in the Borough were employed by the railway companies. Some who were employed in the London offices lived here taking advantage of the reduced fares available to them. This picture shows the large staff employed at Reigate Station in 1900. Today only one man is employed at a semi-derelict station.

In 1864 Reigate Borough Police Force was established. Taken outside the new Police Station in 1912 the picture shows the force of 2 superintendents, 4 sergeants and 26 constables.

Chief Constable W.H. Beacher, the last Chief Constable before the force was taken over by the County Constabulary.

Redhill Fire Brigade seen with their horse-drawn appliance in 1906. The brigades of Redhill and Reigate were independent until 1909 when they merged.

In May 1901, a disastrous fire completely destroyed Nicholls Store at the corner of the High Street and Station Road. Two employees lost their lives. The newly built Wheatsheaf Hotel opposite was slightly damaged.

Reigate Post Office Staff in 1909. The staff of 46 was much smaller than that of Redhill which had the large regional sorting office (see Chapter 2).

The Old Wheel, Luncheon and Tea House occupied a seventeenth century building in Church Street. It drew people into Reigate from a wide area.

Both Reigate and Redhill developed as shopping centres. James Knight & Sons dominates Bell Street. The picture was taken in 1983, its centenary year.

Inside the Old Wheel. Miss Milbourne, seated in the corner, was a gracious hostess. She died suddenly about 1960 and the tea house closed. The site has now been redeveloped.

W. Rose carried on a business as fruiterer and florist in London Road, Redhill. Produce was brought from the gardens of The Frenches in the cart on the left. The picture was taken about 1880.

A little nearer the cross-roads was the business of G.R. Smith established in 1864. He sold china, glass and earthenware. Much of his stock came to Redhill Station from the Staffordshire Potteries.

Pendereds in Station Road West was a well-known Ladies' Outfitter. This picture, taken in the nineteen twenties, shows the windows crammed with goods. This family firm moved further up the road to more modern premises and was demolished to make way for the Belfry Shopping Centre.

The House of Quality

Founded in 1878 by W. P. EASTMOND.

SITUATED IN THE CENTRE OF
Station Road, REDHILL.
Wm. E. TANNER
GOLDSMITH. .·. WATCHMAKER.

THIS fine modern establishment carries one of the best stocks of Gold and Silver Goods to be found outside of London, and is noted for Quality and Low Prices. Practical Men sent to all parts of the county for repairs to House and Church Clocks.

'PHONE 151 REDHILL.

Rebuilt in 1913 by Wm. E. TANNER.

Also in Station Road was the old established shop of William E. Tanner, goldsmith and watchmaker. Above the shop was a large clock which has now gone.

W.A. Buckland, the founder of the well known furtniture shop is seen with two of his men resting after conducting a removal in this late nineteenth century picture.

Windsor Spice Ltd., Photo, Redhill

TELEPHONE: REDHILL 398 and 533

W. A. BUCKLAND & SONS

Removals   *Warehousing*
and Complete House Furnishers
and Cabinet Makers

UPHOLSTERERS

7 & 9 THE PAVEMENT, REDHILL, Surrey

Our Motto: "ALWAYS MOVING"

An old photograph accompanies this advertisement. Much of the stock is displayed outside on
The Pavement. Today the business is run by the great grandsons of the founder.

Hall and Co., Coal, Coke and Builders Merchants, were established in Merstham in 1824. This old steam wagon was used to pull the trucks replacing horses. Later, Hall & Co had yards at both Redhill and Reigate Stations.

Seven
People and Events

Sir Jeremiah Colman who lived at Gatton Hall from 1888 to his death in 1942. He was a great benefactor, particularly to Redhill. He maintained his estate in immaculate condition. The orchid in his button-hole is from his collection which was world famous.

Lady Henry Somerset was the only child of the last Lord Somers and she became Lord of the Manor after her father's death in 1883. She was passionately interested in the Temperance Movement and opened a home for inebriate women and their children at Duxhurst just to the south of the Borough. She spent much time there and is seen here in nurse's uniform. She died in 1905.

The wrought iron gates of Reigate Priory with stone columns surmounted by eagles were erected in 1720. They were removed to a new site on the west side of the Priory building away from Bell Street where there was a Public House which Lady Henry found distasteful. They have been restored recently. The Priory is now a school.

The Priory was often let. King Edward VII was a visitor in 1905. Mr Arthur Balfour, the Prime Minister, stands behind him on the left. The ladies are dressed expensively in long, full dresses and elaborate hats.

This striking picture shows the nine sons of Ebenezer Hooper who came from Bermondsey in 1854 to take over the Tannery in Linkfield Street. In the centre is the eldest son, Thomas Rowland, who remained in Redhill as an architect and surveyor after the rest of the family had dispersed. One of his sons, Dr Wilfred Hooper, became a solicitor and local historian. His daughter, Miriam, was a gifted artist as was his grandson, George.

The wedding photograph of Mr William Tanner, a Redhill business man, in 1902. It shows another selection of the dresses and hats of the time. Notice the bonnet and lace shawl of the older lady on the right.

In contrast is the wedding group of Mr Gayford in the nineteen twenties. Skirts of the ladies are now short and they are all wearing the fashionable "cloche" hats.

A group at the christening of Nellie Bonny outside Bonny Cottage on Reigate Heath in 1906. Three generations of the family are represented. The baby (Mrs Basting) still lives at the cottage.

The Redhill Brass Band in 1912. It took part in the many processions which were a feature of the time. They were to collect money for various charities such as the hospital.

An outing to Oxford by the members of the Reigate & Redhill Chamber of Commerce in 1912. They have paused for a break at Sunbury Lock on the Thames. Almost everybody wears a hat.

One such procession was in aid of the National Lifeboat Institution in 1907. The band can be seen in the rear. Notice the collecting bags at the end of long rods.

A crowd has gathered in Castlefield Road for the opening of the Public Baths in 1906. They were erected through the generosity of Mr J B Crosfield. Notice the school boys wearing knee breeches, stiff collars and caps.

A group arriving at field where the tableaux were judged. The winner was local artist Mr Tatton Winter, a son-in-law of T. R. Hooper.

A memorable event in 1913 was the Pilgrims' Pageant organised as a fund raising event for the purchase of Colley Hill. The groups who took part represented scenes from Chaucer's Canterbury Tales. A Prioress is seen in the centre of the picture. People lined the route from the top of Colley Hill to a field in St. Alban's Road.

At the outbreak of War in 1914, many men volunteered to join the army. These recruits are lined up near Chart Lane.

A scene in the centre of Reigate where crowds gathered to cheer the troops on their way from Aldershot to Folkestone for embarkation to France.

A Scout Rally in Gatton Park in the 1930s is being addressed by Lord Baden Powell, the Chief Scout, who founded the movement.

The War Memorial at Shaw's Corner in 1923. Admiral of the Fleet, Earl Beatty, who lived at Reigate Priory is seen in front of the Memorial at its dedication ceremony.

The fifth Redhill Girl Guides. The six patrol leaders are grouped round their Captain, Miss Gwen Gosling, in 1936.

Redhill Football Club founded in 1894 played on the Sports Ground in their distinctive red & white striped shirts. A pavilion was opened in 1898 by Sir Jeremiah Colman whose interest made it possible.

Processions still took place after the War. The Chamber of Commerce organised an annual Carnival. Many traders produced decorated floats. Here the Carnival Queen, surrounded by her attendants is being crowned by the Mayoress, Mrs Spranger in Reigate Town Centre.

The Redhill eleven in 1906 - 1907. They played in the Athenian League from 1923 to 1984 when the Sports Ground was closed. The Club moved to Kiln Brow to a less satisfactory pitch on Weald Clay which is easily water-logged. The Sports Ground is now a public park.

Redhill Madrigal Singers. Joyce Hooper holds the B.B.C. Rose Bowl (SE section) won in 1964. The singers were one of the many musical groups in the Borough.

Standing in front of the scenery are recognisable characters. Henry VIII and his six wives with Cardinal Wolsey on the right.

Many Pageants were held in the Priory grounds produced by Cecile Hummel. One in 1953 was in celebration of the Queen's Coronation while that in 1963 was to commemorate the Borough Centenary. In this picture, some of the characters are assembling.

Chief Constable W. H. Beacher is surrounded by his Tug-o-War team in 1932. Trophies they have won are set out before them.

A group of skaters on the ice of Gatton Park lake in the severe Winter of 1940. The leader of the 'crocodile' is Mr S. Goss. Outdoor skating is now rare as indoor rinks cater for a more sophisticated clientele.

Another crowd gathers to see the Delta Airship which came down in a field adjoining Masons Bridge Road in 1910. It was repaired and sent on its way the next day. After accidents to the R100 and R101 in the 1930s the development of such lighter-than-air craft was abandoned.